IF YOU DISCOVER A FIRE

SHAUN ROBINSON

Brick Books

Library and Archives Canada Cataloguing in Publication

Title: If you discover a fire / Shaun Robinson.
Names: Robinson, Shaun, 1980– author.
Description: Poems.
Identifiers: Canadiana (print) 20190238348 | Canadiana (ebook) 20190238380 |
ISBN 9781771315272 (softcover) | ISBN 9781771315289 (HTML) | ISBN 9781771315296 (PDF)
Classification: LCC PS8635.O2638 I3 2020 | DDC C811/.6—dc23

We acknowledge the Canada Council for the Arts, the Government of Canada through the Canada Book Fund, and the Ontario Arts Council for their support of our publishing program.

Canada Council for the Arts Conseil des arts du Canada Canadä ONTARIO ARTS COUNCIL CONSEIL DES ARTS DE L'ONTARIO

The author photo was taken by Rossanne Clamp.
The book is set in Minion Pro.
Design and layout by Marijke Friesen.
Printed and bound by Coach House Printing.

Brick Books
115 Haliburton Road
London, ON
N6K 2Z2

www.brickbooks.ca

For Rossanne and Alannah

TABLE OF CONTENTS

Greyhound Depot, Cache Creek

In the dry-mouthed intermission of a three-act journey
you stand in line and consider your choices:
chalkboard specials and blackened bananas,
hot dogs that bob like pool toys on rollers.

You settle for coffee, for five minutes alone
in the blank stare of a Cache Creek afternoon,
the smell of sagebrush and Mama Burgers.
You're not a smoker, but you feel down

to your last match. In ten years of changing
buses here you've never seen anything change.
The motel pool's still closed for repairs.
The same gap-toothed assortment of stale candy

and travel shampoos in the vending machine.
When only the weekly paper marks time
it's easy to forget that anything happens,
that your parents met here, decades ago,

in the incomprehensible era of Kenny Rogers
and indoor smoking. All you have from that time
are a half-dozen Polaroids tucked in a paperback.
You shuffle through them sometimes like a bad

crib hand, wondering what you could do
without. You have your father's duffel bag
and your mother's laugh, a watch they gave you
when you turned sixteen that's never kept

the right time—3:02 could be 3:05, or midnight,
or 1978. You could turn around and see them
framed in the window, sharing a cigarette
and a plate of fries in the moment they sensed

their future idling at the curb and decided to board.
With no idea that journey's end point would be here,
this wasted hour from which you're trying to salvage
some revelation. But don't bother looking—

you have what you need to get where you're going.
Take a newspaper, maybe, some motel matches.
The highway asks only patience, offers nothing
but time to think about your choices.

Trivia Night

It's important to get things wrong,
even if it feels like fighting
with a lover, forgetting important dates
and the names of her friends,
and she thinks it means you don't care.
We do care, America, just not about
your state parks or your presidents,
the pretty coins stamped with their faces
spinning through the pub's gloom
to settle a bet about the year we landed
on the moon. Remember that, America?
High-fiving the cosmos, trampling
the dusty surface of eternity? Four-hundred-
whatever years after Vasco da Gama
discovered whatever it was—
Florida, maybe, or fire, or the fountain
of youth, which I imagine surrounded
by marble parrots and bubbling
like a vodka soda. It doesn't matter
if it's real. The helicopter has only existed
since 1936. The zipper was invented
in 1891, and before that we lived
without it. Picture Lincoln fumbling
with hooks and loops above a chamber pot
in the Ford Theatre moments before
every fact he's ever known is blown
through a hole in the back of his head.
And the facts in yours will one day rot
into a black soup, the capitals floating
in a stateless void, every letter
of Mississippi emptied into the Gulf.
Isn't that why you come? To test

yourself in the blackout shrine
of a neighbourhood pub, to honour
the knowledge you've lived without?
You know as much as you need to.
Your mother's maiden name, floating
inside you like a slice of lime
in a vodka soda. You know the story
and the shortcut, the password and the prayer.
You know you'll wake on your bathroom
floor, the toilet glowing above you
like a ceramic moon, like a match
struck on your zipper in the dark room
of everything you've forgotten.

Where Do You Bury the Survivors?

Sometimes I think you're a fox
and I'm trying to row you across
a river. You're also, for some
reason, a chicken and a bag
of corn, and I only have room
in my boat for one thing
at a time. The river is
this conversation or the river
is the rest of our lives.
Or the river is just a border
between one solid place
and another where we want
to stand together. Not that
I think you're really a fox
or a chicken or a measure
of dead weight—I mean
that I'm afraid if I leave you
alone the parts of you
that seem at odds
will start consuming
one another. And
now I think of another
grade-school riddle: a plane
crashes on a border,
and where do you bury
the survivors? Back then,
we'd say, *You don't*
bury survivors.
But that's not right, is
it? Sometimes you do.

Convenience

Every day I pass
two women who
stand, hands folded,
beside a rack of
pamphlets that read,
Will Suffering End?
They face the all-night
gym, ellipticals
and treadmills
lined up like catapults
in the window.
They say it's madness
repeating the same
action expecting
different results,
yet the bodybuilders
grow stronger and
stronger and the women
marshal an army
of souls to
storm the afterlife.
So if, at two a.m.
every Saturday,
I find myself
at the Mac's on
the corner, deciding
which exotic salt
I want to lick
from my fingers,
don't assume it's
a failure of will—
I go to be soothed

by the timeless
casino light
of the aisles,
the drifting sensation
of easy rock,
like the store
has come unmoored
from the city,
a glass submarine
moving under
the surface of night,
bearing its payload
of soft drinks
and frozen burritos
toward sunrise.
Enemy territory.
The coolers
humming like two
beers into an evening.
The keno board
flashing news
of distant loss.
When I pass the gym
with my hand
jammed in a bag
of Doritos I know
I am kin to the man
stretching himself
on a rack, his face
twisted with regret,
the cords in his neck
as thick and red
as Twizzlers.
It's given to both

of us to do the work
that's done at night.
Tending the flame
of suffering.
Passing it
like a torch
from one day
to the next.

If I Wrote a Poem About My Father

I'd tell you how he taught me to know whitetail
from mule deer by prodding roadkill with his rifle,
north by the moss on trees
and spruce by the pain it caused,
to draw the thin, green capsules of nectar
from Indian paintbrush and a knife
from a trout's gills to its anus, to scoop out
the sloppy coil of intestines,
the soggy raisin of its heart.
I wouldn't have to explain how
the intimate, animal smell of his work clothes
occupied the laundry room or how his greasy
orange-shelled chainsaw ruled the basement
perched on its tarped pile of firewood
and board ends. If I said he once went
behind our house and attacked
the hillside with mattock and shovel,
carving it into a series of steps
where my mother planted
carrots and sunflowers, I would leave
out the time he tied
my brother's dog, Joey, to a post
and shot him with the .22 because he wouldn't
stop chewing on Pepper's skull.
I'd tell you that he taught me to layer
kindling over balled paper, light it in
several places and let the flame
build before adding logs, but not that he had scars
all over his arms from lighting himself on fire.
And if I said I still build fires the way
he taught me, I wouldn't mention
how the rain and the years washed out

the terraces he made behind the house.
I wouldn't say that he still
has his scars, that I'm still on fire.

Punxsutawney Bill

What has no shadow has no strength to live.
—Czeslaw Milosz

Someday someone's going to see me interviewing
a groundhog and think I don't have a future.
—Phil Connors, *Groundhog Day*

Across the courtyard, a smoke alarm yaps
like a purse dog. He could close
the window, but after thirty-four years
trapped in the snow globe of a single day

it feels good to let the spring in—tiny birds
like living chimes woven into trees,
blossoms unfolding intricate odours.
The day used to be a pop song

and he knew every note. Now
it's a horror score—the alarm shrieks
like the strings in *Psycho*.
Car horns are jump scares.

Unrinsed cans and cutlery clog
the kitchen sink. Fruit flies
strafe the compost. No one tidies
while he sleeps anymore,

unsnapping pencils, dusting
snow from lawns. Nor are his still-burning
mistakes snuffed out by the heel
of whatever force it was he lived under.

Toilet paper rolls shrivel
like the snowbanks behind
the hockey rink. He considers walking
to the mall, which, with its permanent

sales and light of endless afternoon
is more familiar than anywhere else.
Instead, he pours vodka on ice.
When Rita discovered he'd only ever learned

the one piano medley, the one
French poem, she stopped taking calls.
"I'm like a magician's rabbit," he tells
his reflection in the toaster,

"adjusting to life outside the hat."
He could always go back
to the land of polka and no
cappuccinos—an hour and change

on the highway. But no,
that place has lost its magic, too.
It's the hat hung back
on its hook—*the living soul*

has dribbled away, like his ice sculptures
melting into gravel.
Far off, to the east, wisps
of cirrus begin to gather. He used to know

what that meant. The alarm is becoming
a new present, a background track for eternity.
At least he knows now that, given time,
he could learn to hear it as song.

Tyler, You're Terrific

Tyler, you're useless. Your hands hang off
the ends of your arms like a couple of starfish
you found on the beach. When you argue with
the waitress, you sputter like a shaken Coke.
She calls you *Dear*, the same word strangers
use when they write letters reminding you what
you owe them. Pay attention, Tyler. A flamingo
without its *o* is just flaming.
Library books and babies both have
due dates, but don't confuse them.
And don't assume a fire drill is a tool
that bores through steel with flame.
It's an orderly exit from a building, Tyler.
And if I tell you to tear up your life
and start over, remember some things
are made whole by destruction. A kernel
of popcorn is useless until it explodes.
And Tyler, if I tell you you're terrific,
remember the root of the word is terror.

Sunomono

Just because the sun is a globe
of orange fire and not an orange
soda is no reason not to enjoy
your morning. Even in a vacant lot,
dandelions are framed, like art,
by old foundations. And whether
or not they're worth something,
the pennies in your pocket chime
like a tambourine, adding
a pleasing brightness to your day,
like the half-moon of lemon
in sunomono. The building I live in
is made of two-by-fours and trembles
when a train passes as if it's receiving
a message, and yet I'd rather live
here than downtown, where
the wall of glass towers looks less
like a city than a shelf of high-end
vodkas, unless it's the tiny city inside
the cracked-open television
in the alley where I leave
my empties. A sign there reads
Waste Only, which seems
like a hard way to live.

Pilgrims

As we drove it down the stairwell
Curtis's couch bucked and fought
like a rodeo bull in its chute, shedding dust
and dribbling a trail of coins and cushions.
Downstairs, we tried to wedge it
into a U-Haul packed with everything
we'd carried that day: his grandfather's chairs,
his mother's linens, his Craigslist bookshelves.
The five of us who'd come to help Curtis
ferry his life across the city were silent.
Bryce lit a cigarette, sat down on a kitchen chair
among the boxes and suitcases scattered
around the parking lot. "It's not going to happen,"
he said, and I knew he was right—the single
trip we'd planned would turn into two, and none
of the things I'd meant to do with the rest
of the day would get done. What those things
were, I wasn't sure, but I knew
that whatever was wrong in my life I would
have fixed that afternoon. Instead, I travelled
with Curtis from Kitsilano to East Van,
balancing a model boat on my lap, trying
not to snap its delicate rigging as I turned
the dial in search of hockey-draft updates.
Half of what Curtis had gathered in twenty-four
years rode behind us, unsettled,
shifting on corners. I spent the day
shouldering duffels of laundry and angling
tables into elevators, wiping sweat, downing
water, cradling the bottoms of overloaded
boxes of books and kitchen utensils. The more
I carried the less I saw the use of any of it.

And because I forgot the ship in the cab
of the truck I had to carry it back across
the city twice more. I resolved one day
to trim my life back until it fit in the matchbox
hold of that vessel. It was only hours
later, carrying the ship up
to the new apartment, setting it
on the bookshelf, that I saw it was
the *Mayflower.* We were pilgrims, I thought,
and it didn't matter what we'd carried—
we'd crossed the ocean of another day
and found a new shore.

Shared Accommodation

In the room for rent, a phone
cable leads the eye out
of the frame. Beds are seen
through half-closed doorways,

as if they were shameful. Stains suggest
indecent acts but might be shadows.
Small pets okay. Close to bus routes,
in the sense that everything is

close to bus routes. We're all in
our late twenties—quiet, respectful,
employed. We enjoy activities
unclear at this resolution.

Ignore the photos on the fridge—
that's who you'll be replacing.
Temporary is okay, in the sense
that everything is temporary and okay.

New Year's Day

I wake up in a friend's Mile End apartment.
Noon, and even the leaves have gone home
for Christmas. The only food I can find
is in jars—crunchy peanut butter
and purple sauerkraut. I rustle through
a paper sack of bagels, stale souvenir zeros.
There's a bruise on my thigh the shape
of Haida Gwaii. I could probe its depths,
if I wanted, chart the *X* of what hurts
against the *Y* of how much, use the data
to reconstruct the sidewalk that did
the damage, calculate speed and direction,
fill in some empty spaces. If I wanted.

Instead, I follow a craving for bitter coffee
down Saint-Laurent, limping around
unfenced construction sites and party debris.
Red plastic beer cups are symbols
that need no translation. I snap cellphone
photos of *À louer* signs in low-rise windows.
Two weeks in Québec and still crashing
on couches, still lost whenever I surface
from a Métro station, my inner compass
useless without a mountain horizon. By the time
I find coffee, my body is making new demands,
for ibuprofen and food-court Thai.

I have no choice—I obey. Why not?
It was impulse that brought me here, farther
from home than I've ever been. Later tonight,
I'll ride the Métro for hours, from Beaubien
to Côte-Vertu, from Snowdon to Jean-Talon,

rattling under the dense weave of city,
streets and habits, names and wires laid down
in a grid of meaning. When I finally arrive at Peel,
two blocks from my destination, a busker in the station
will be playing "Hallelujah," and as usual,
thank god, he'll be getting it all wrong.

The Future Lives Here

I spent the summer copiloting a pickup
though Surrey, trying to interpret
a binder of ancient Parks maps—
impossible in a city whose motto
was *The Future Lives Here.*
Where the map showed a cornfield
we found a full-grown subdivision,
four-storey townhouses repeating
like wallpaper, the same swing set
and toppled big wheel in every yard.
It didn't help that Garret, my boss,
popped ephedrine to stay awake
and only knew east from west
by tapping out *Never Eat Shredded Wheat*
on the wheel. From seven to four
we hopped from park to park to loop
rubber mats around the trunks of city trees.
The mats smelled like the insides
of galoshes and had to do with mowers
or moisture retention or something.
I didn't mind the work, but Garret
never shut up except to dribble chew
into a Big Gulp cup between his knees,
rambling in a sports-bar grammar
of hockey fights and hangovers. At twenty-nine,
he had two kids by different women.
The longest he'd ever been faithful
was to an annual pass at the gym.
I couldn't believe I'd moved to the city
to be trapped in a truck
with this Prince George hick,
a dead ringer for every man I'd known

in seventeen small-town years.
So why did I meet him every Friday
at a downtown pub to sip from
seven-dollar pitchers and listen
to his lectures on real estate
or his keno system while he sighted
down his cue at a gridlock
of stripes and solids? Something always
went wrong, an eight that refused
to go down or light up, but he swore
one day he'd run the table
and haul his winnings to Costa Rica.
I couldn't stand to hear him talk
about the future as if it existed,
but it was better than my tiny apartment,
twilight guttering in the slice
of sky you could see from my only window,
framed by towers that threatened
to extinguish everything. If only
I could have spent my nights
in the calm of the moment after we'd set
the final mat of the day:
the sod cut away and replaced
with a black circle, the grass and soil
swept off, three staples to hold it
in place. The moment it all fit together
as if I'd never been there.

Versus Nature

Regret, zeroed by the onset of fall,
recurs in its minor key. The day creaks
open like a lid on no sleep at all.
On the stove the kettle rattles and shakes
like a rocket taking off. Out there, trees
stand heartbroken, nude, and geese, offended,
get up and leave. Your Honour, if it please
the court, this line will show the defendant
glowed through the night like a candle and kept
himself awake. Exhibit A: a pile
of ceramic shards, flecked with bran flakes, swept
under a chair. The kettle comes to boil,
and light like flat ale in a shaker glass
presses against the window and won't pass.

Stereognostic

In colours of pants unknown to nature,
in impractical canvas shoes, the poem falls
in love. The poem leans in romantic repose
against the fourth wall, picking its teeth
with a wooden match. I want it to know the names
of city flowers, but all I know are city squirrels
and low-born daffodils. I want the poem to
sink into unguent, the word itself, how the moan of *ng*
is trapped like a calf in a swamp of gooey *u*.
I want the poem to be a list of the foods
that remind me of you, just as I am a list
of the foods that make me forget you.
Instead, the poem is everything that unfolds
from smaller shape to larger, every fabric
that turns out to be too thin to keep the daylight in.
I crumple it and touch it to my lips.
I want to wrap my heart in the damp poem
and microwave it on low for thirty seconds.
And I want to know the poem the way
all across the nation, in back yards
and rec rooms, piñatas spill their candy souls
to their torturers—that is to say, I want to know it
the way the kids with sticks know where to swing.

Balcony

Gulls accumulate on the neighbour's lawn.
Their calls have always struck you
as insincere, like the cries
of hired lamenters.

You wanted a garden, but settled
for a view, as furniture settles
into carpet, consoling yourself
with a few pots on the balcony.

The basil, fighting something,
blackens at its edges.
The cherry tomato has climbed
six feet through the balcony's light

and still not found what it needs,
but it keeps climbing.

The Cop-Shop Deer

Daytime, the sidewalks belong to pigeons
that look glued together from chopsticks
and dirty napkins, but come sunset
the cop-shop deer creep out from the ditch
beside the Mounties' parking lot, sliding
like shadows across storefronts—the gem shop
three years into its going-out-of-business
sale, a hand-scrawled *Help Wanted* sign
at the liquor store, where what's wanted
cannot in good conscience be called help.
Their hides ragged as welcome mats,
bearing their nerves and their ticks
from the bridge to the sawmill, they spook
at the sprinkler's rattlesnake shiver,
leap like fountain water across
the split-rail to crop new tulips
from the library lawn. They graze beside
the motel pool, stiffen into lawn chairs
when a Doberman shakes the fence.
Like marmots hiding from coal trucks
under cattle guards, they shelter under
the steel grate of law, though when they slip
into the trailer park to gum tomatoes
from a wooden trellis they think no more
of their fate than the infant just inside the window,
burbling the night away like a crock-pot.
Before they cross the highway, they touch
a hoof to its surface as though it were ice.
Cracks spread through the silence,
but nothing breaks.

Your Love Will Help a Child in Need

The key to stacking creamers
is a steady hand, which I don't have.
My structures crumble like Corinthian
columns. Alannah and Phoebe's
art-school minds turn everything
to sculpture, moments stacked
one by one until they topple.
Can art that isn't boring arise
from boredom? Probably not.
You could try to interpret plastic flowers,
unlocking meaning with keys cut
from context, from theory, but why
bother? The simplest lock and key
are bottle and opener, or so it seemed
last night, a house party somewhere
off Clark, the air full of smoke, music
transmitted bone to bone, too useful
to be art. In Alannah's most beautiful
photograph, Phoebe sits on the floor
of her old apartment, legs folded,
eyes slightly sad, slightly bored.
When a shadow is underexposed,
whatever it held is lost to time.
Alannah and Phoebe believe in things
like that, in time and space.
They conjure futures from charts
and flames, and once flew to Texas
for $126, a price so low it demands
interpretation. When the food arrives,
sculptures are swept aside,
affirming a hierarchy of needs.
Unlocking my omelette with knife

and fork, I am grateful for cream
in coffee, for homemade hot sauce,
its useful pain that reminds me
of the man last night who waved
his fingers through a lighter's flame
in an act of boredom and defiance.
I was on the bus, the night receding
to a fixed point in a realistic gesture.
If you believe in time, you might believe
Alannah and I were once in love,
though in the moment, which is all
that exists, we eat breakfast.

Carpe Dos and Carpe Don'ts (ft. Panda Bear)

Well, when you try to seize it, the day
turns to sand. And the moment is too little
living space, a broom closet inscribed
on a grain of rice. You've searched for it
for thirty-two years, but it's buried
somewhere deep in the sand on the beach
of all your wasted days. The only time
that exists is the Summer of 2013, a time
so dope that Mayan philosophers glimpsed it
in a collective dream and invented
paradise and apocalypse. And as for
those lemons, the ones life gave you once—
the Summer of 2013 saunters into your kitchen
and takes them from your hands, slices them
into sixths, pulling a bottle of Patrón
and a shaker of salt from a pocket.
Out on the porch, between shots, he tells you
things you've always known, how the past
and the future are lovers spooning
in bed, and the present is how they don't
quite fit together. For instance, he says,
take that moon, and then he does,
plucking it out of the sky like a lemon
from a tree. It's not a moon at all,
it never was: it's the prettiest moment
you've ever seen, big as a beach ball, skin
as thin as a nectarine's. You could do anything
in a moment like that—you could fall
asleep in a pile of warm laundry.
You could call your estranged mother
or roller skate over a burning bridge.
And now the Summer of 2013 is lifting it

over his head. And now he's bringing it down
across the railing, and now it splits open
and the juice trickles out, the unadulterated
juice of authentic, one-hundred-percent-real
time. And now he's filling his cupped palms,
he's lifting them to your mouth, and he whispers,
Now that's what I call lemonade.

You're Fine, Tyler

I understand desire, Tyler.
I've been to the dog park,
seen the retriever's face
flap like a flag as it pursues
the *idée fixe* of the tennis ball.
But say a cop yells *Freeze*
while you're on an escalator.
What do you do, Tyler?
An octopus in a jar can learn
to unscrew the lid, so why can't you?
You used to think ball pits
were fun and girls were gross.
Now it's the other way around,
but that's the only thing
that's changed. Think about it.
Before you assemble the puzzle
someone has to cut it into pieces.
I didn't say you were like
a fine wine, Tyler. I said
Stop whining, you're fine.

Where to Find Help When

Dead spruce stand like coat racks
on a brown carpet of flattened grass
in the world's most barren
hotel lobby, but you couldn't pay me to stay here,
not at this time of year, and Benjamin drops
into fourth to pass a logging truck,
one pine wobbling like a lance
aimed dead at my chest
as we roar uphill. When I travel home
it's always through mountains,
always uphill, reluctant
as Hamlet returning from his studies
to the absence of a father.
Ben knows the twelve-hour drive
like a pop song—its good and bad
stretches, its dreary repetitions,
the call and response of speed limit
and brake light—but the morning was clogged
with rental RVs and oversized loads,
a swarm of soccer players
at A&W, and we're making up
for lost time. I ask him, "Would your father's spirit
really say, *I am thy father's spirit*?
Wouldn't it say, *Hi, son*?" He claims
he's never seen the play.
Fine, but he's seen *The Lion King*.
He's seen his father's face appear as a cloud
of mosquitoes above the North Saskatchewan.
We pass without stopping through towns
that lie at low points along the highway,
as if they'd lost momentum
and came to a rest, full of fathers who lost

momentum and came to a rest,
fathers riding the clutch
into their fifties, fathers who brood
over the ashes of the barbeque pit, who sing
Journey at bowling-alley karaoke, trying to hold on
to a feeling that fades like a centerfold
tacked above the tool bench in the garage.
And Ben and I fly by in our father cosplay
of flannel and facial hair,
obeying the paternal advice
of local radio, which warns of wolves
and avalanches, which says
to keep moving.
In my wallet, I have a page torn
from a motel Bible
that reads *Where to Find Help When*,
and when I'm weary of dragging
my father's ghost through the mountains
like a load of logs,
when I am sleepless or envious,
tempted or broken-hearted,
I take comfort in the coordinates
of help even without a book
in which to seek it.
On long straight stretches, Benjamin
tilts back his head to nurse
a trickle of sweetness from two frozen liters
of No Name ginger ale.
He props his clutch foot on the dash,
letting the gears bear us along like a river.

How Soon, How Likely, How Severe

The first day, the fire climbed the slash
like a jungle gym and leapt to the canopy.
We dug out eight kilometers of hand line
where the slope was too steep for the Cat.
I snapped a Pulaski and ground
my palms to burger. Thank god we're not
a dry camp. The next three days
the pump rattled like a Datsun cresting
the Coquihalla, sucking from the pond
until the shallows quivered with a jelly
of tadpoles. We bound the fire in two-inch hose
and bare soil and called it contained.
If anyone asks, Kamloops, the fire is contained.
We spend our overtime among the black spires
of burnt fir, sniffing for the socks-on-the-
camp-stove scent of smoldering duff.
I wake up pawing the motel carpet
for hot spots. A voice on the handheld asks
if I remember my old life. I remember
ground fire creeping from root to root,
approaching an interface with the unspoken.
A threat under the surface. Now, I could load
my duffel into a chopper and fly, nose down,
along the seam of the present tense.
Self-sufficient for twenty-four hours
with a bird's-eye view of the point of ignition.

Disaster Preparedness

> *PLANNING FOR THE FUTURE IS ESCAPISM.*
>
> —Jenny Holzer

The night wears the moon
like a headlamp, checking the city's
expiry date, drunk students
rolling around like batteries
in a drawer as their bus mounts
the suspension bridge,
its cables a graph
of probabilities. A monument
to risk. They travel inland,
away from the red zone of tidal surge
and structural failure, while I
walk home from a party
where disco lights set an aquarium castle
aflame and the goldfish flitted
from turret to turret failing
to put it out. The two friends I'd come with
found their way to a couch, wrapping
themselves around one another
like emergency blankets,
so I talked for an hour to an architect
who told me his earthquake kit
is a helicopter.
They say you need three days'
worth of what you need,
but I don't even know what that is
on a day that hasn't fallen apart.
I need a closet the size
of a thrift store in which to climb
through the luggage and rubble

of other lives. I need coffee
in a paper cup and enough blocks
of the city to circle until
my feet hurt.
I need to see my friends
in the bar full of old couches,
playing the game
where a card on your forehead
says what you are. Last time Dom
was Venice, sinking slowly
into the upholstery.
I was either a god or a ghost
or an astronaut. *Am I famous?*
I asked my friends. *Am I still alive?*
Can you walk around inside me?
Right now I'm a ghost for sure,
haunting Broadway, a strip
of empty buildings fragile
as teacups in a cupboard.
I'm drifting toward
my apartment where the pipes
moan like flexing stone,
the windows rattle
in their frames whenever
my neighbour gets laid.
At the party, I left the architect
in his disastrous kitchen
and stepped onto the balcony
like stepping onto a stage
before an audience of thousands.
The towers dressed
in black, lights glinting
like gold watches.
I felt alive and famous.

I felt disaster walking around
inside me. When morning roars to life
like a generator, you'll find me
braced in the doorway,
another *x*-ed off day on a calendar
counting down to some unknown hour.

Material Safety

This product may cause eye irritation
if for some reason you spray it
in your eye. It rates a 4 as a fire hazard.
The scale is unspecified. At some point
if you keep injecting it into a rat
the rat will die. Does knowing that
make you feel any better?
Symptoms of inhalation are dizziness, excitation,
euphoria and incoordination, and if that sounds
less like a warning than a good night off,
I don't know what to tell you.
This product smells like propane,
though propane actually has no odour.
Its scent of homemade sauerkraut
is an additive, an engineering measure
in case of accidental release.
One of those phrases that produces
a kind of disaster-movie thrill.
Repeat the words *eye protection*
until you believe in eye protection.
Put faith in cool, well-ventilated rooms.
But honestly, why do you bother?
Even table salt has an LD50.
If boredom does, it hasn't yet been
isolated—colourless, odourless,
caustic as lye, it melts
in empty time like sugar,
suspended between seconds.
There are no countermeasures
with which to combat it,
nor any other immaterial danger—
the flickering sadness

transmitted by subtle movements
on a screen, the poverty to which,
like a childhood home, you always return.

Annie, Annie, Are You Okay?

> *The body consisted of a spring metal hoop which simulated the ribs, and provided the foundation for the chest upon which compressions could be done.... Between classes, the body was deflated, and Anne was folded and returned to her storage box.*
>
> —The Virtual EMS Museum

Day after day, I die in the mailroom's
manila light, my arteries clogged
like a paper tray. I'm flattened by a forklift
called boredom in the empty warehouse
of Wednesday afternoon. It's slapstick
in its repetition. You're probably bored too,
lulled by the drone of instruction, senses
wrapped in gauze, checking and rechecking
the clock's vitals, having pumped on my chest
so long you know the creak and give of my ribs
like an old mattress. Thoughts drifting
past the window, past business hours,
as the second hand thrusts uselessly against
the flatlined present, waiting forever for help
to arrive, as the manual instructs.
From the corner of my eye I can see
the on-ramp that leads to elsewhere,
the cables of the suspension bridge. I'd kill
to fall, just once, from its railing, a lonely note
plucked from a harp. If you really want to help,
before I'm folded and put away like a shirt,
let me drown in a mall fountain, coughing up quarters
like a slot machine on the food-court tiles.
Or, if my heart is destined to be my locus of failure,
let it fail outdoors, on a sidewalk, say,
on the public stage—traffic parting like a curtain

at the ambulance's approach.
Sirens building to a standing ovation.

We Must Now Accept All Evidence Suggests

To the light that's turned out, it's the room
that has vanished, to the balloon as it rises,
pursued by its tail of string, the sky is the new present,
disappear is the past tense of a child's hand.
A hand is open and a phone continues to ring,
analysts fail to prove it is not the same balloon
launched by the Japanese in 1944 carrying
an incendiary charge that drifted to the suburbs
of Detroit but did not explode, they fail to prove
that in French a light is *closed*,
not turned off, that the witnesses' composite drawing
of D. B. Cooper has not been mistaken
in the lineup for a stamp of Matías Pérez. In the airport
lounge the unanswered ring takes on the meaning
lost by *Arrival* and *Departure*, by the string
of numbers below. To vanish is now the text,
loved ones are exegesis. The ring is like holding
an ocean to your ear and hearing an empty shell.

Year of the Monkey

A man on a ladder attacks a building
with a machine that emits a wedge
of sparks and a smell like driving
with the parking brake on. And you
want to know if I can be more
casual? It depends on the weather,
on whether an overcast sky
is more like a waiting-room ceiling
or the surface of a scum-covered pool.
It's true the clouds resemble
a flotilla of empty milk jugs bobbing
back and forth across a shallow
sky, but the truth bears only a casual
relation to appearance—the man
I said was attacking a building
was sanding a section of awning tube
to make its surface rougher
and more adherent. If I told you that,
you'd roll your eyes and put your hand
in my pocket. I want to be more transparent
in my desires, to hand you a Ring Pop
and ask you to love me as long as it lasts,
maybe a little longer. Keep an open mind
is what I'm saying, pencil in a line
of a poem in which we drive
from Marfa, Texas, to Baton Rouge.
In the meantime, I'll settle for Chinatown
buck-a-shuck. It's wonderful and awful,
don't you think, to slurp down an entire
existence without chewing? The truth is
a certain amount of surface roughness
is necessary. When I say, for example,

"The clouds look as if they're trying to empty
their emptiness onto our existence,"
and you answer, "I wish they would."

New England Epithalamium

All morning the weather objected, pounding the fist
of itself on traffic and awnings, claiming that it
had loved the landscape first, that it was the valley's
father. Where the streets flooded, rings of water
rippled over the pavement, exchanging themselves

over and over, until the drunk storm collapsed
behind the bandstand. Oh, why can't I marry
America, its colleges wearing white, its rains
that believe in the literal truth of the Bible?
In the Quaker Church we are solemn as laws.

The bride glows like a Yankee candle,
and the groom is the shadow she casts.
The vows are simple: "Instead of a ring, I promise
the years will be as dense as diamonds.
For our paper anniversary, I'll throw you a parade

and cover you with confetti." The priest mumbles
a mouthful of polyamorous Latin verbs
and suddenly we're dancing on the lawn, where the vows
our laces made to themselves come undone,
and we move barefoot among the wasps eloping

with fallen peaches. We raise our glasses
in common prayer to the bottle of reposado,
while the bridesmaid rolls around behind the chapel
with a local whiskey and the sun pulls an Irish
goodbye, slipping shyly past the horizon.

Tuesday

You're the week's little finger,
like soul night at a metal bar.
A collect call on a tin-can telephone.
A moth's moonlight complexion, mistaking
patio lanterns for love. I see you dating
a man who keeps his suits zipped into
garment bags as if they wanted
to escape. With a bar across your eyes
in the background of the atrocity.
When the car pulls out of its spot,
the square of dry pavement where
the rain hasn't fallen but soon will.

Student Night

Students wait for student night
at a bar that throbs like a bad liver.
Umbrellas graph a correlation
between patience and desire,

of which I have neither.
I only know what I don't want—
I don't want sour cream in my burrito.
I don't want to move to Hawaii.

I couldn't stand the tropics—the day
sliced in half like an avocado,
the afternoon an empty green hole
where the pit used to be. Some pits

are holes, but the ones in avocados
are tiny mahogany moons.
The real moon looks like ricotta.
The sea looks like a beat-up Volvo,

like it's travelled a half-million miles
and still not arrived.

Halftime

In the first half our linebackers handled
like hand-me-down Econolines.
The uprights were tight as tuning forks.
When helmets clatter like billiard balls,
I guess one might get sunk.
One wide receiver went so long
he exited the building, flying past
the ticket takers and tailgaters.
He ended up merging onto the highway,
always looking over his shoulder
like someone in witness protection.
But that was the past, an unrecoverable fumble.
The future unspools along a ruler
made of grass. Help will not come
from the sideline refs, those nihilistic pylons
who see the world in black and white,
and the playbook is nothing more
than a doctoral thesis on tic-tac-toe.
The only good news: the hairline fracture
in the kicker's ankle turned out to be
an eyelash on the x-ray.
And now we'll make our own news—
edit our destiny inch by inch,
or let the quarterback etch a single line
of poetry, and hope the receiver
understands. Look how eternity waits
at the end of a tunnel, how the blimps,
convinced they're manmade clouds,
have started to rain.

Terminal

By a series of oversights and moving
sidewalks I've arrived at a place without
Advil or legroom. A view
of what could be Ohio or Oregon.
Like the flight attendant's smile,
it offers little. The book I'm reading,
commands me *Live immediately*,
a difficult task under the turbulent
regime of the seat-belt sign, hips
in the vice of armrests. Nor could I obey
an hour ago, defeated
by the liminal space of the tarmac,
its cryptic lights and de-icing stations,
where I lost faith that my baggage
would find its destination. I pictured
a suitcase tumbling out of a chute
in Houston, circling the carousel
like a child forgotten at the fair.
The book is called *On the Shortness
of Life*. Life has never felt longer,
especially compared to the stir stick
that circles the coffee cup twice
and ends its gnat-like existence
in the bottom of a garbage bag.
The whole future lies in uncertainty,
writes Seneca. As if knowing that
makes any difference.

Frozen Waffles

I staggered out of my room
like I'd been stabbed, clutching my phone
as if it could provide a clue
to my killer's identity.

The day had popped out of the toaster
warm as a waffle, and the sun
had the blank, hopeful expression
of the one *Survivor* contestant
who *is* there to make friends.

I found a half-finished crossword
on the tank of a public toilet
and carried it under my arm
until I felt incomplete.

As if the day were destined
to be a series of puzzling failures.

For an hour, I watched two clouds
collide, advancing in increments
like fist-bumping glaciers or scholars
coming to a consensus. At three p.m.,

I reached the midpoint of my existence.
I was alone in a strange city called
my life, officially too old
to ever become a cool dad.

I hadn't tried to hide, but I wasn't easy
to find. If I could have retraced

my steps, I would have left a trail
of clues, like a fairy-tale child
abandoned in the woods, in the hope
that someone would follow.

Clues like Five Across, *A tree disguised
as a box to sneak into the back yard*,
or Twenty-Six Down, a three-letter word
for *Business noose*.

To get home from here, I'll follow
the truck watering city flowers,
past storefronts where mannequins stand
with their hips cocked like shortstops
between pitches.

Package Gravy

The park smells like freshly showered
evergreens and secret vomit.
A man with a rake takes his cigarette break
under an alder sapling. Its foliage
a puff of green smoke. You want to find
something to eat, but I only think about lunch

in the slapdash grammar of bachelor cuisine—
package gravy and government cheese,
the spreading of various things on toast.
And if I don't always know
who I'm speaking to, at least

I've convinced myself the microwave's
keypad resembles a face.
We walk past angle-parked cars
grazing on parking meters like bison
that don't know they've only been saved
from extinction to serve
as gourmet burger patties.

I'd like to think if we kept walking we could escape
the tangle of building codes and traffic lights
we call the city, but it goes on and on
like a boring dinner date.
It ends somewhere to the east, where the ocean
sits quivering in its bowl

like an ancient and inedible desert.

The Man Who Took Photos of Windows

In one, a life is laid out in the form of watches and fishing tackle, a dented trumpet,
a Coleman stove, a trio of medals from World War II. It was taken
in 1957, in a city that isn't there anymore, even if some of the windows are,
like the one where a woman stands in an open aperture of floral drapes,
the words *Bargain Shop* above her, and behind her nothing at all. It's easy to see
why he took them: the windows were already photos, frame and all,
though no one else noticed at the time. There's one

where a cedar box is being torn up for concrete forms, and another
where a fifty-cent top has just begun to spin—it later became a Kodachrome tornado
that rolled down Granville Street, sucking up cigarette butts and bits
of bloody tissue paper. When he took a photo of his West End room, it showed
the window, toothbrush and safety razor on the sill, the same razor
used by the man in the window of a Main Street diner, whose features
are blurred but whose fear is as plain as the words on a menu.

I Used to Walk Around With a Tiny Forest

If I go outside, the wind will steal
my hat, so cancel all my sunsets
and lattes. The city looks ransacked.
Trees shaken down for their leaves,
newspaper boxes knocked over, sandwich
boards scattered like playing cards.
These slow, hypnotic dusks convince me
never to eat without the television on.
I said I wouldn't go out, but here I am.
I have a bag of laundry, an almost aquiline
nose that would look good on money.
I like to live within the scent of the ocean.
I like harbours, even unsafe ones.
I like to see raw tonnage calm as stone
in the water, cranes unloading cubes
of wind and medicine. When I don't wash
my laundry I feel like a negligent landlord.
On some streets, the power's out, on others
it may as well be. Houses hide
behind hedges, timid as moles.
A pair of cedars in someone's yard
surrounded by trimmings, like men
in a barbershop. Just up the block,
a barber cuts hair by candlelight.
If only my clothes could be cleaned
the same way, trained hands
searching fabric by the light
of a tiny flame, snipping out flaws.
When I arrive at the laundromat,
the door will be locked, the machines
silent. There's nothing as still
as a washer that's done thumping

the dirt from a load of towels.
The heart must wish for that kind of rest,
tired of shoving its unbalanced load
through the circulatory system, as tired
as I am of hauling dirty clothes
around the city. When I was younger
I carried a tiny forest in a pair of bags
on my hips, wandering through the aftermath
of catastrophe, wondering where
I should put it. Somewhere to the west,
I think I decided, where the pink of sunset
would complement the green needles.
I wonder what it's grown into,
what it might harbour.

Try Harder, Tyler

An ice machine is a tiny factory, Tyler.
It sits in the hotel's industrial district,
beside the elevators and vending machine,
turning tap water into ice cubes
to chill the drinks of paying guests.
And what do you do, Tyler, with what
you've been given? This morning
I thought I saw a scarecrow's burlap face
staring through my bedroom window,
but it was a wasps' nest stuck in the limbs
of the neighbour's tree like an evil football.
A wasps' nest is also a factory, Tyler.
It manufactures wasps. It's harmless now,
but all summer it worked away, unseen,
pumping out malice like a paper heart.

Ash Wednesday, Kingsgate Mall

Half an hour before closing, a man
croons into the urinal, swivelling his hips
as he empties his bladder, ecstatic with relief.
He knows the future is made of vodka
and Coca-Cola because it's waiting,
already mixed, beside the sink. I pray
one day I'll find something I love as much
as this man does pissing, but for now I walk
the empty corridor, through the scent
of floor wax and minimum wage, past the florist's
imprisoned blossoms, mistaking myself
for a stranger in the hairdresser's dim mirror.
I've come to the mall for paper towel,
but now I'm at the liquor store, reading the labels
of blended Scotches while the clerk reads Hegel,
plotting to smash the state like a bottle.
We all make plans, I guess. Like my friend Bryce,
who's given up alcohol for Lent, stocking up
on San Pellegrino, jewel-toned sodas
all the sweeter laced with the bitterness of sacrifice.
I know we are contained by vessels, by shoelaces
and short-term leases, the B-Line drifting
down Broadway's churning traffic.
My wallet contains a cheque, signed and dated
like a bottle of good whiskey. The cheque
contains the last two weeks of my life.
I'm studying the shelves, deciding how much
of my past I'll give up, which future I want
to carry home under stars as clear as vodka,
a sky as black and sparkling as Coca-Cola.

Chelsea Motel

A man on the sidewalk carries a chair on his head
like a set of cast-iron antlers. It must be nice
to always have somewhere to sit, though hard
on the neck. I probably look that awkward
bearing my clumsy love through all these doorways
and Tuesdays, trying not to get tangled in awnings.
If it were fabric, I'd drape it over my arm to save you
a seat in the restaurant. It's weird, Chelsea.
Whenever I text to ask what I should order,
my phone changes Malbec to becalm, like a bartender
saying I've had one too many. Let's settle
for Caesars and hope they don't turn into race cars
by the time they get to the table. Back at my motel,
there's a sign on the wall that starts a sentence
with *If you discover a fire* and ends it with a map.
As if fire were some new Florida and we were at sea
on a queen-sized raft. But you can find fire
anywhere, Chelsea. If you ask at the desk,
they'll give you a book of matches.
And the waiter is moving from table to table
with a lighter and a candle.

Intimate Mechanical Forces

The cook steps out of the kitchen
bearing a steel bowl of fries, its rim
salted like a margarita, while someone,
somewhere, drowns in a swimming pool,
as five hundred and eighty-seven people do
in an average year. It's nearly midnight,
and Prime Time Chicken's television
is muted and tuned to hockey.
Someone has died of exposure
in the time you've stood at the counter.
Someone has fallen from a ladder
or structure, but the two-piece combo,
with gravy and fries, costs the same
as a three-zone fare at the bus stop
across the street. You've taken that bus as far
as it will go, smelling of beer and lurching
like a nightclub, through suburbs
repeating their dog parks and civic centers
like small talk, blinds flashing blue
with the intimate light of basic cable,
the people inside who will die
from overexertion or contact
with inanimate mechanical forces.
In Prime Time's duct-taped booths,
the men wear hoods and study
their plates like sacred texts.
Fish and chips and broccoli beef,
runny lasagna, cheese pizza, food so oily
you turn a half-dozen napkins transparent
with grief every time you visit.
And while people choke and fly
through windshields and disappear

into cataclysmic storms, you thumb
the wheel of your lighter. A man
wipes his beard with his sleeve.
You begin to think that you've made
a mistake, the way I did a few lines back,
writing *grief* instead of *grease*.
Don't worry. This isn't the kind of place
where anyone will notice.

Transactive Memory

We met in a bar the width
of a hallway leading nowhere.
You asked me my sign in a neutral
tone. I covered my mouth
with a placemat when I yawned.
I read to you from a book
of burnt-out matches.

You said you didn't want to put
labels on it, but I'd just bought
a label maker. You looked at a fern.
You opened the fridge. You described
your past as a reluctant ode
to Shoppers Drug Mart. I fell
asleep in a pile of sporting goods.

For years I worked under the table,
that one from the phrase *farm to table,*
while you wrote a thesis on transit anger.
We argued like agnostics resorting
to prayer. You asked, "When does
The Wire get good?" I felt complicit
in your library fines.

You drifted into your thirties
like a polar bear on an iceberg.
I wouldn't stop yelling *Enhance!*
at the view from the kitchen
window. At night I translated
my sorrow bump by bump
from the Braille of a bucket of Lego.

I pursued an aesthetic impulse
into the suburbs. The train slid
over the rooftops like a runaway
attic suite. I curled up inside my fear
like a tuba player in his instrument.
The sky stripped off its blue negligee.
A voice told me where I was.

You waited with your signal on
for the intersection to clear.
I tended to the campfire of my vices.
On a road trip, you vanished
into the space between rest stops.
When you came back, you spoke
authentic American boredom.
You buried bulbs with a tiny shovel.

You scrubbed the floor like a storm
erasing the names from a map.
I invested my bingo winnings
in abstract pornography.
We fought in parking lots
where pigeons shuffled around
like hungry slippers.

The city, at night, was roofed
in blue light. The rain seemed
to fall from a stadium ceiling.
We whispered our Wi-Fi password
to the flowers. At midnight, a thousand
coupons expired in a drawer and ivy
climbed the walls like slow, green flame.

NOTES

The italicized phrase in "Punxsutawney Bill" is from Elizabeth Bishop's poem "Crusoe in England." The epigraph quotes Czeslaw Milosz's "Faith," translated by Robert Hass.

The title of "We Must Now Accept All Evidence Suggests" is from a text message sent by Malaysia Airlines to the family members of passengers lost on flight MH370.

The epigraph to "Disaster Preparedness" is from Jenny Holzer's *Truisms.*

The epigraph to "Annie, Annie, Are You Okay?" quotes Mark Peck's article "Annie . . . Annie . . . Are You OK? Resusci Anne" from The Virtual EMS Museum.

"Terminal" quotes C. D. N. Costa's translation of the essay "On the Shortness of Life" by Lucius Annaeus Seneca.

"The Man Who Took Photos of Windows" references the photography of Fred Herzog.

ACKNOWLEDGMENTS

Some of these poems first appeared in the following publications: *Arc Poetry Magazine, Bad Nudes, The Puritan, Echolocation, Prairie Fire, The Malahat Review, The Rusty Toque, NewPoetry.ca, The Maynard* and *Poetry Is Dead*. My deepest gratitude to their editors. Thank you, as well, to Shane Neilson and Caryl Peters at Frog Hollow Press, where some of these poems also appeared in the chapbook *Manmade Clouds* and the anthology *The City Series: Vancouver.*

I was fortunate to have many teachers during the writing of this book. I'm grateful to Amber Dawn, Ian Williams, Karen Solie, Rhea Tregebov and Sheryda Warrener for the time I spent with them.

Thank you to my editor, John Barton, and to everyone at Brick, for their patience and care in guiding this book to its final stages.

I've also been fortunate to be a part of the most vibrant and supportive writing community I can imagine. Thank you to everyone who has been a part of it, and especially to Mallory, Curtis, Kayla, Adèle, Dom, Selina, Jess, Megan, Rachel, Jocelyn, Carter, Kyle, Chris and Mica.

SHAUN ROBINSON'S poetry has appeared in *The Puritan*, *The Malahat Review*, *Prairie Fire*, *Poetry Is Dead* and *The Rusty Toque*, and received Honourable Mention in *Arc Poetry Magazine*'s 2018 Poem of the Year contest. Born in 100 Mile House, BC, Robinson has lived in Vancouver since 2006. He studied in UBC's Creative Writing MFA program, where he served as the poetry editor of PRISM *international*. He is also the author of the chapbook *Manmade Clouds* and currently works as an editor for the chapbook press Rahila's Ghost. *If You Discover a Fire* is his debut collection.